BOBA FETT

THE LEGEND LIVES

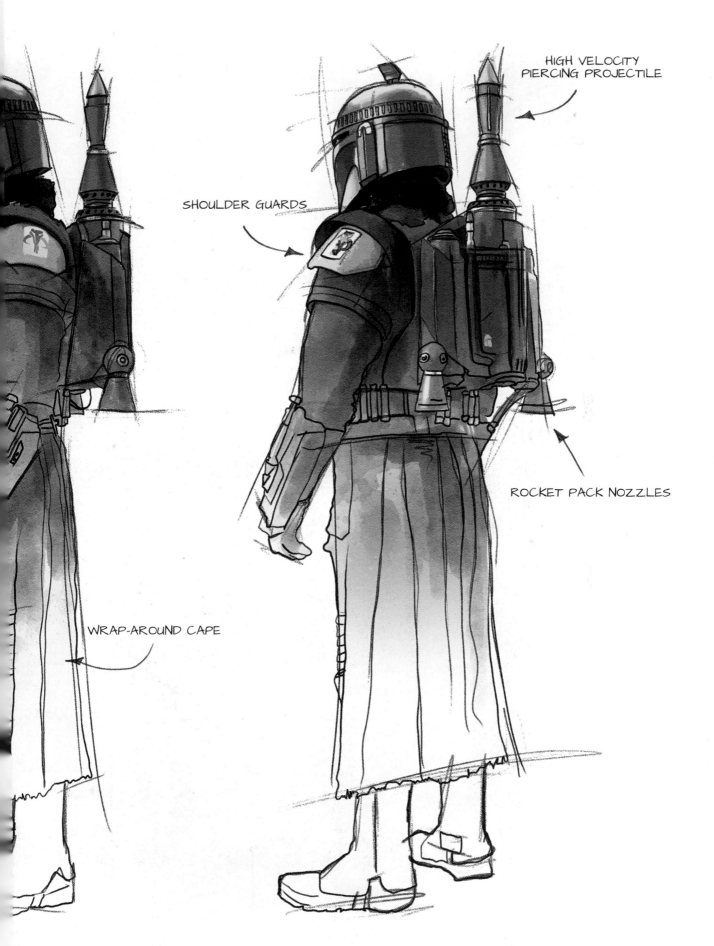

HIGH VELOCITY
PIERCING PROJECTILE

SHOULDER GUARDS

ROCKET PACK NOZZLES

WRAP-AROUND CAPE

© LFL

UNTY HUNTER

THE CENTER SEAT 6

ELITE MERCENARY

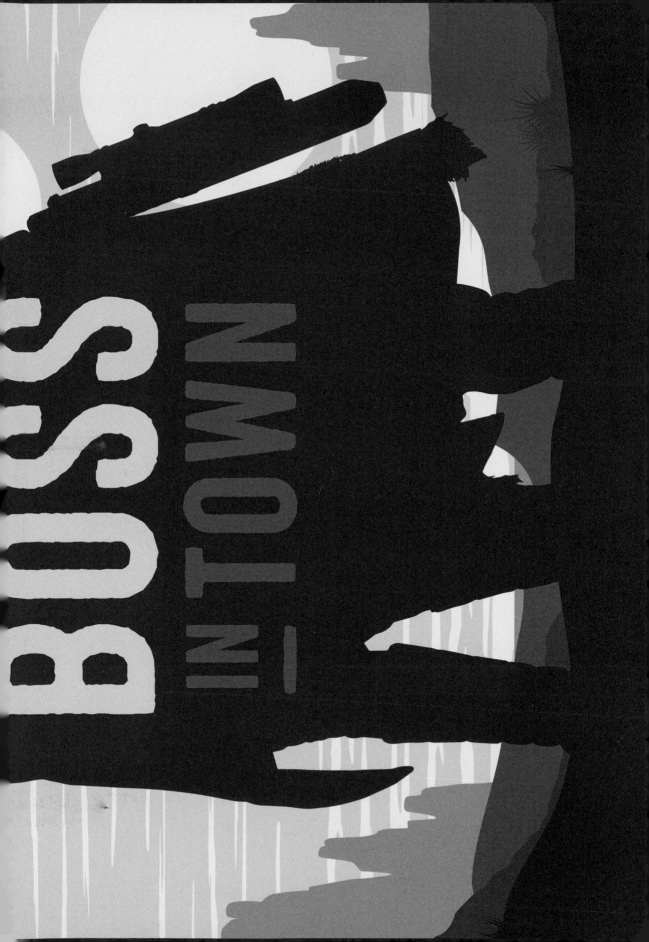

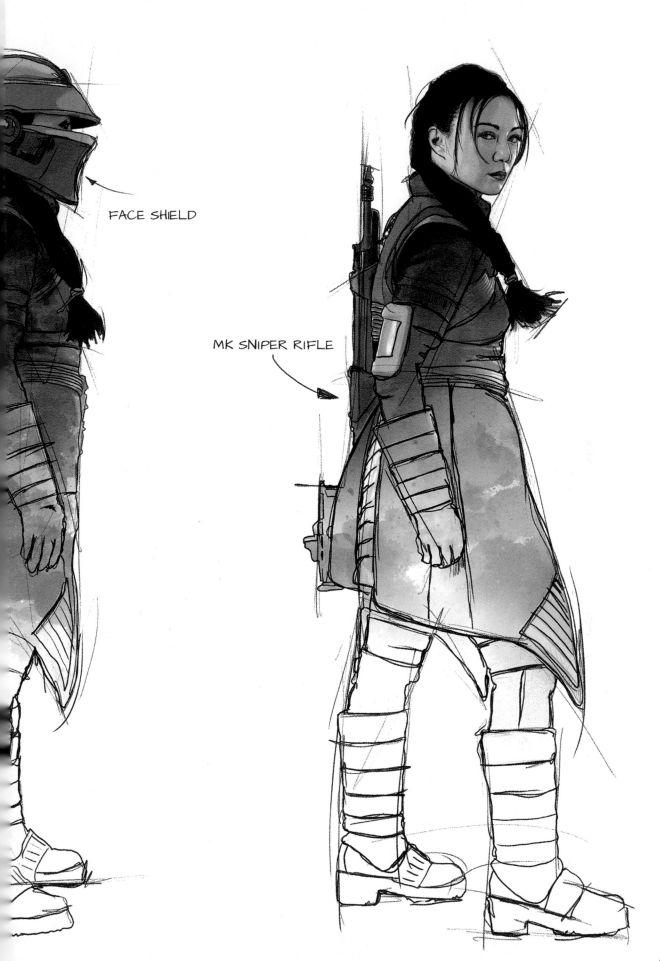

FACE SHIELD

MK SNIPER RIFLE

ION CANNON (CONCEALED)

CONCEALED TURRET WITH TRACTOR BEAM PROJECTOR
AND TWO PROTON TORPEDO LAUNCHERS

Boba Fett

Firespr

BOARDING RAMP (RETRACTED)

ARMORED HOUSING FOR DRIVE SYSTEM

SENSOR JAMMER (CONCEALED)

STABILIZER FIN

COCKPIT

MAIN THRUSTERS

SENSOR ARRAY

REPULSOR GENERATOR

ION CANNON (CONCEALED)

CONCUSSION MISSILE LAUNCHER (CONCEALED)

WEAPON ACCESS PANEL

ROTATING TWIN BLASTER CANNONS

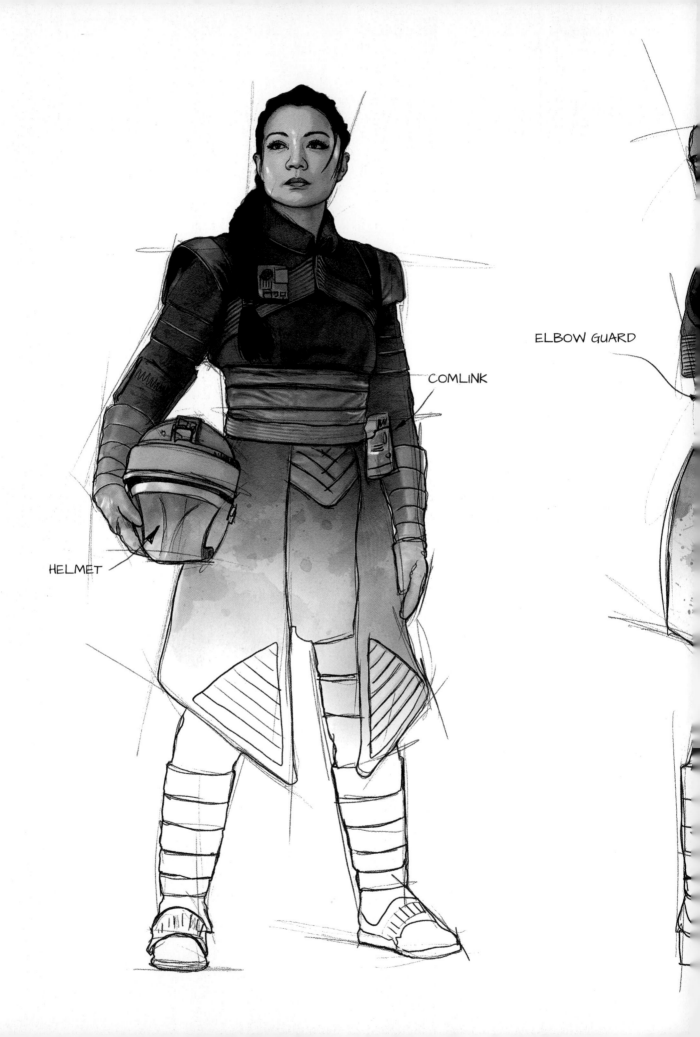

ELBOW GUARD

COMLINK

HELMET

THERE'S A NEW

LEGENDARY B

RANGEFINDER READOUT

DENT

INFARED VIEWPLATE

BATTERY UTILITY
BELT

MULTI-DIRECTIONAL
ROCKET DARTS